# LET'S EXPLORE SCIENCE

# Water & Floating

## David Evans and Claudette Williams

**DORLING KINDERSLEY**
LONDON • NEW YORK • STUTTGART

# A DORLING KINDERSLEY BOOK

**Project Editor** Dawn Sirett
**Art Editor** Karen Fielding
**Managing Editor** Jane Yorke
**Managing Art Editor** Chris Scollen
**Production** Jayne Wood
**Photography by** Susanna Price
**U.S. Editor** B. Alison Weir

First American Edition, 1993
2 4 6 8 10 9 7 5 3 1

Published in the United States by
Dorling Kindersley, Inc., 232 Madison Avenue
New York, New York 10016

**Library of Congress Cataloging-in-Publication Data**

Evans, David, 1937–
     Water and floating / David Evans, Claudette Williams. -- 1st American ed.
        p.  cm. -- (Let's explore science)
     Includes index.
     Summary: Uses simple observations and experiments to explore the properties
of water.
     ISBN 1-56458-208-6
     1. Water--Juvenile literature.   2. Water--Experiments--Juvenile literature.
[1. Water-Experiments.   2. Experiments.]
I. Williams, Claudette. II. Title.  III. Series.
QC145.24.E67  1993
532--dc20
                                                                    92-53479
                                                                       CIP
                                                                       AC

Reproduced by J. Film Process Singapore Pte., Ltd.
Printed and bound in Belgium by Proost

Dorling Kindersley would like to thank the following for their help in producing
this book: Daniel Pangbourne and Dave King (for additional photography);
Coral Mula (for safety symbol artwork); Mark Richards (for jacket design);
Julia Fletcher; and the Franklin Delano Roosevelt School, London.
Dorling Kindersley would also like to give special thanks to the following for
appearing in this book: Natalie Agada; Sammy Arias; Hannah Capleton;
Sapphire Elia; Foyzul Kadir; Tony Locke; Gemma Loke; Rachael Malicki;
Paul Miller; Kim Ng; Maxwell Ralph; Daniel Sach; Anthony Singh;
Ahmani Vidal-Simon; and George Woolgrove.

# Contents

# Note to parents and teachers

Young children are forever asking questions about the things they see, touch, hear, smell, and taste. The **Let's Explore Science** series aims to foster children's natural curiosity and encourages them to use their senses to find out about science. Each book features a variety of experiments based on one topic, which draw on a young child's everyday experiences. By investigating familiar activities, such as bouncing a ball, making cakes, or clapping hands, young children will learn that science plays an important part in the world around them.

## Investigative approach

Young children can only begin to understand science if they are stimulated to think and to find out for themselves. For these reasons, an open-ended questioning approach is used in the **Let's Explore Science** books and, wherever possible, results of experiments are not shown. Children are encouraged to make their own scientific discoveries and to interpret them according to their own ideas. This investigative approach to learning makes science exciting and not just about acquiring "facts." This way of learning will assist children in many areas of their education.

## Using the books

Before starting an experiment, check the text and pictures to ensure that you have gathered all necessary equipment. Allow children to help in this process and to suggest materials to use. Once ready, it is important to let children decide how to carry out the experiment and what the result means to them. You can help by asking questions, such as, "What do you think will happen?" or "What did you do?"

## Household equipment

All the experiments can be carried out easily at home. In most cases, inexpensive household objects and materials are used.

## Guide to experiments

The *Guide to experiments* on pages 28-29 is intended to help parents, teachers, or helpers using this book with children. It gives an outline of the scientific principles underlying the experiments, includes useful tips for carrying out the activities, suggests alternative equipment to use, and additional activities to try.

## Safe experimenting

This symbol appears next to experiments where children may require adult supervision or assistance, for example, when they are heating things or using sharp tools.

## About this book

**Water and Floating** enables children to investigate the nature of water and other liquids. The experiments demonstrate that water can exist in different states, i.e., solid (ice), liquid (water), or gas (steam), and that each of these states has different properties. Children will find out that:

- some liquids mix with water and some solids dissolve in water;

- liquids can flow, fill the shape of a container, form drops, and wet surfaces;

- liquids will find their own level when left;

- liquids exert upward forces that prevent objects from sinking, unless those objects can exert greater forces downward;

- when an object moves on or through water, friction occurs and tries to prevent that object from moving forward (this friction can be reduced by altering the shape of the object);

- dirty water can be made clean and that plants and animals need clean water if they are to stay healthy.

With your help, young children will enjoy exploring the world of science and discover that finding out is fun.

**David Evans and Claudette Williams**

# What is water like?

What does water taste, smell, feel, and sound like?

**Looking and smelling**
What does water look like? What does water smell like?

**Looking at water level**
Hold a bottle of water at different angles. Does the level of the water stay the same?

fizzy mineral water

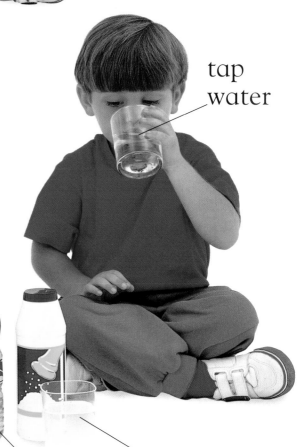

tap water

**Tasting**
Does mineral water taste the same as tap water? What does water taste like when you add salt to it?

still mineral water

salty water

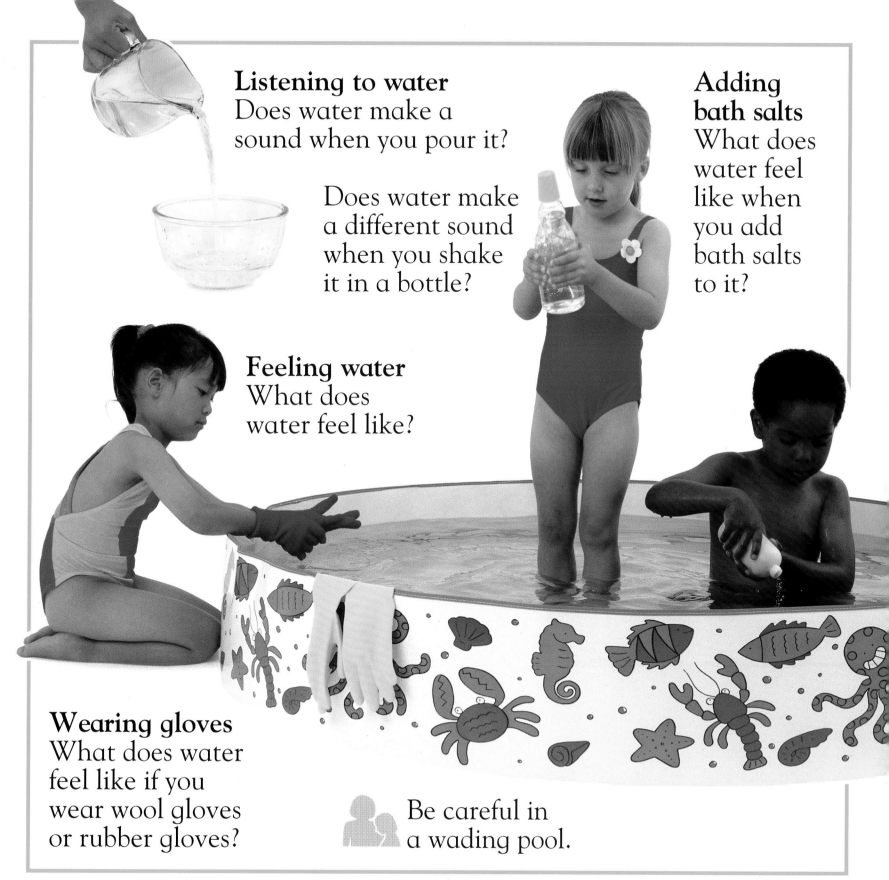

**Listening to water**
Does water make a sound when you pour it?

Does water make a different sound when you shake it in a bottle?

**Adding bath salts**
What does water feel like when you add bath salts to it?

**Feeling water**
What does water feel like?

**Wearing gloves**
What does water feel like if you wear wool gloves or rubber gloves?

Be careful in a wading pool.

11

# Will it mix with water?

What things will mix with water?
What will mix with other liquids?

Do not taste the liquids.

**Liquids**
What different liquids can you find around your house?

vegetable oil

vinegar

syrup

perfume

water

dish-washing liquid

Is water a liquid? Is syrup a liquid? Is vegetable oil a liquid?

Do all liquids smell the same?
Do all liquids pour?

## Mixtures

Try adding some of the things on this page to water. What do you see? Which ones dissolve? What will happen if you stir the mixtures with a spoon or a beater?

## Drops

What happens when you add a drop of food coloring to water?

vegetable oil and bath salts

rice

water

baking powder

vinegar

flour

milk

butter

brown sugar

bath salts

Shake some vegetable oil and bath salts in a jar for a long time. What happens?

What happens when you add baking powder to vinegar?

# Is water always a liquid?

Try these experiments to find out
if water is always a liquid.

### Cold water

What will happen if
you leave water in a
freezer overnight?

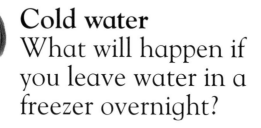

### Cold bottle

Leave
a bottle
in a refrigerator
for an hour.
What happens
to the bottle
when you
take it out?

### Cold mirror

Put a hand mirror in the fridge. Leave
it for an hour. What happens when
you hold the cold mirror over a warm drink?

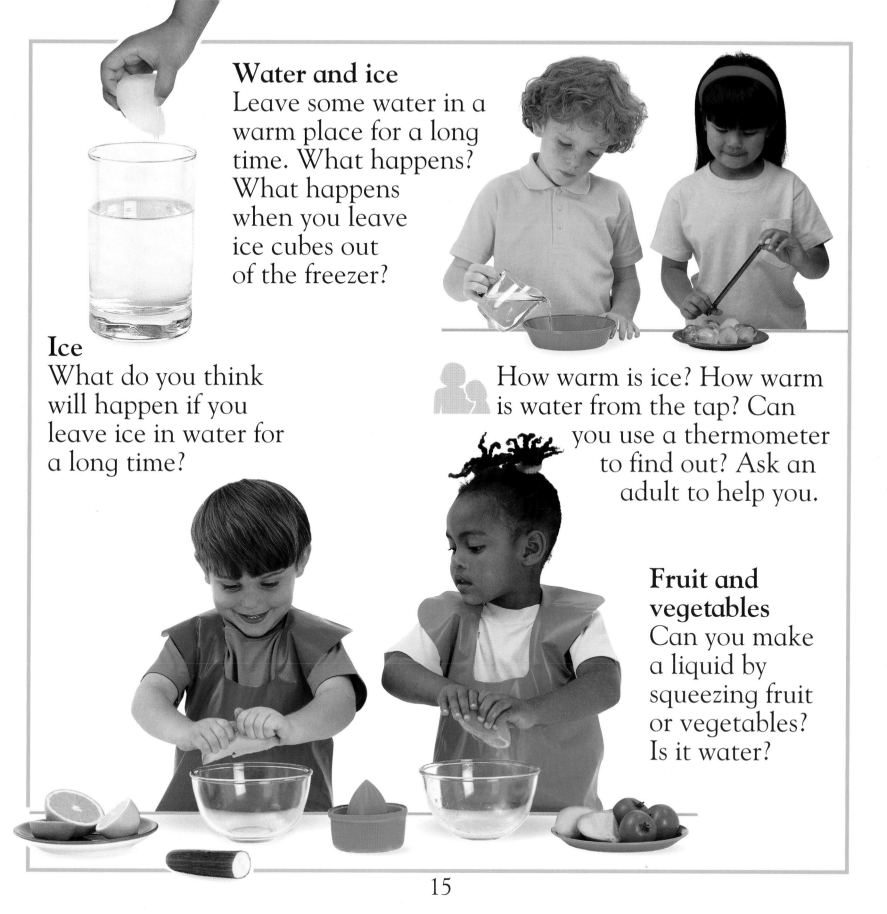

## Water and ice
Leave some water in a warm place for a long time. What happens? What happens when you leave ice cubes out of the freezer?

## Ice
What do you think will happen if you leave ice in water for a long time?

How warm is ice? How warm is water from the tap? Can you use a thermometer to find out? Ask an adult to help you.

## Fruit and vegetables
Can you make a liquid by squeezing fruit or vegetables? Is it water?

15

# What shape is water?

Can you change the shape of water?

**Water in a bag**
Ask an adult to help you fill a plastic bag with water. How can you change its shape?

**Frozen water**
Does frozen water look the same as liquid water? Does it feel the same? Can you change the shape of frozen water?

Wear gloves when feeling frozen water.

**Drip race**
Put drops of water, dish-washing liquid, or vegetable oil on a mirror.

Which liquid will run down the mirror fastest?

16

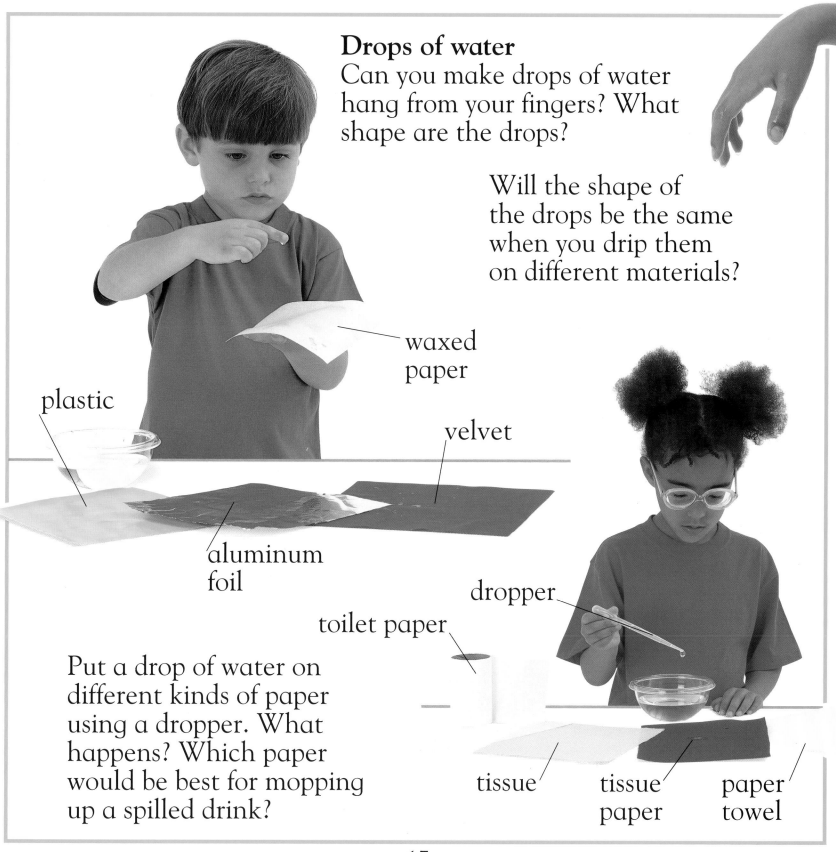

**Drops of water**

Can you make drops of water hang from your fingers? What shape are the drops?

Will the shape of the drops be the same when you drip them on different materials?

waxed paper

plastic

velvet

aluminum foil

dropper

toilet paper

Put a drop of water on different kinds of paper using a dropper. What happens? Which paper would be best for mopping up a spilled drink?

tissue

tissue paper

paper towel

17

# Can you fill it with water?

How quickly can you fill and empty different things?

### Filling bottles

Put some empty plastic bottles into water. Which one fills up fastest?

### Filling with a jug

Can you use a jug of water to fill some bottles? Is it easier to fill the bottles if you use a funnel?

### Emptying a jug

How many cups can you fill with one jug of water?

## Filling cups

Try putting plastic cups into water at different angles. Do they always fill with water?

Put a plastic cup under water. Turn the cup upside down and slowly lift it out of the tank. What happens?

## Emptying bottles

Ask an adult to help you make some holes like these in plastic bottles.

Fill each bottle with water. Which bottle empties fastest? What happens if you keep your hand over the top of the bottle?

19

# Can you move water?

Can you move water from one place to another?

**With a straw**
Can you move water using a drinking straw?

**With a spoon**
Can you move water using a spoon? What happens if you use a strainer?

**With your hands**
Can you move water using one hand? Is it easier with two hands?

What other things can you find that will move water?

## With a tube
Fill a tube with water. Use a funnel to help you.

What happens if you lift one end of the tube?

## With bottles
Can you move water using a squeeze bottle or a spray bottle?

## With a siphon
 Hold a tube under water so that it fills up with water. Leave one end of the tube in the water. Put your hand over the other end and lift it out of the water.

What happens when you hold this end of the tube over a lower bowl and take your hand away?

What happens if the two bowls are at the same level?

# Will it float on water?

Find some different objects to drop into water. Can you guess which ones will float?

**Floating objects**
What will happen when you drop your objects into water? Will they float or will they sink?

Drop a hard-boiled egg and an uncooked egg into the water. What happens?

## Ice
Do you think ice will float in these different liquids?

water

salty water

syrup

vegetable oil

## Table-tennis ball
Hold a table-tennis ball under water. What does it feel like? What happens when you let go of the ball?

## Plastic bowl
How many ways can you find to make a plastic bowl sink?

## Modeling clay
Can you make a piece of modeling clay float? Can you make it sink?

# Will it move in water?

Try these experiments to see if you can make things move in water.

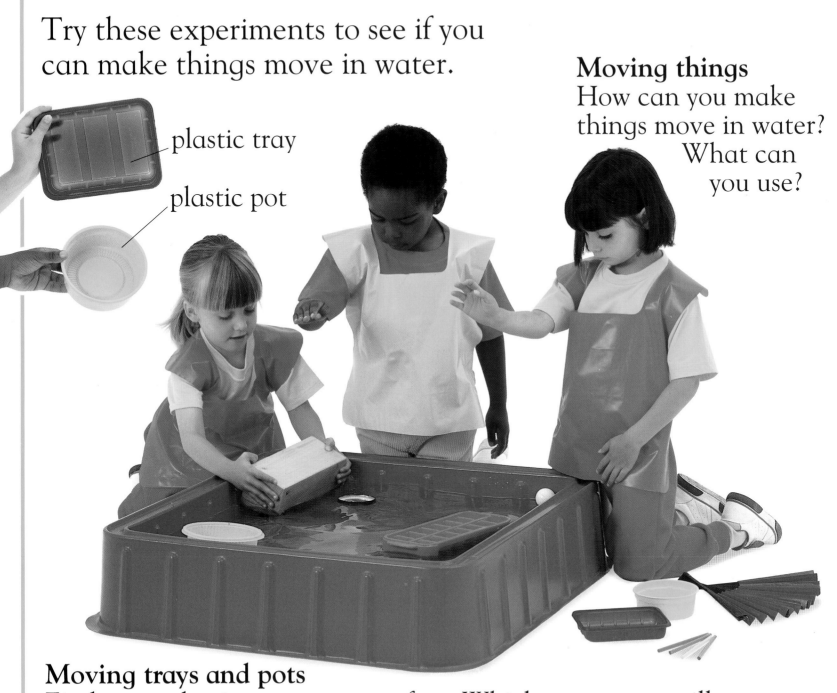

plastic tray

plastic pot

**Moving things**
How can you make things move in water? What can you use?

**Moving trays and pots**
Find some plastic trays or pots of different shapes to use as boats.

Which tray or pot will move through the water fastest?

24

paper
sail

toothpicks

modeling clay — cork

## Making a cork boat

Make a cork boat. Put it in water. Can
you blow it over? What happens if you
attach a bigger piece of modeling clay
to the bottom of the boat?

## Sailing boats

Make a sailboat using paper,
a plastic tray, modeling clay,
and a popsicle stick. Which shape
of sail makes your boat go fastest?

Are two
sails better
than one?

# Can you clean water?

Can you make water dirty using some soil? Can you make it clean again?

 Wear gloves when doing these experiments and do not drink the water.

## Gravel filter

Can you make a gravel filter? What happens to dirty water when you pour it into the gravel filter?

## Filters

Can you use a colander, a sieve, or a coffee-filter paper to clean dirty water? Which one cleans dirty water best?

## Cloth filter

Set up two bowls and a washcloth like this.

washcloth

empty bowl

dirty water

What happens to the dirty water? Now try using paper towels or cotton instead.

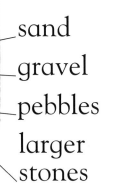

sand

gravel

pebbles

larger stones

wool

paper towel

**Different materials**
Spoon some dirty water onto different materials. Which material cleans dirty water best?

muslin    plastic    cotton

Which material would you use for a raincoat to keep you dry?

**Aquarium**
Can you think of some plants and animals that need clean water to live in?

When do you use clean water?

# Index

# Guide to experiments

The notes below briefly outline the scientific principles underlying the experiments and include suggestions for alternative equipment to use and activities to try.

## What is water like? 10-11

Using their senses of touch, taste, smell, sight, and hearing, children explore the properties of water. They find that water is a colorless liquid that does not have a strong taste or smell.

## Will it mix with water? 12-13

Here children start by comparing the properties of various liquids. By pouring the liquids, children discover that liquids flow at different rates. Children could also be asked to look at the way salt or flour flows and to decide if these substances are liquids. Adding a range of solids and other liquids to water helps children understand that some solids dissolve in water and some liquids mix with water.

## Is water always a liquid? 14-15

Water is shown to change from a liquid to a solid, or from a gas to a liquid. Water vapor in the air condenses into water on the cold bottle and mirror. Children could also watch an adult hold a metal spoon in the steam from a boiling kettle and observe the steam condensing into liquid water on the cold spoon. When children leave water in a warm place, it evaporates. By squeezing liquids from fruit or vegetables, children can begin to appreciate that living things contain large amounts of water.

## What shape is water? 16-17

Here children discover that liquid water flows and spreads, but ice doesn't. They also examine water drops and find that they "cling" to some materials, but are absorbed by others.

## Can you fill it with water? 18-19

Children learn about capacity by filling and emptying containers. When emptying bottles with holes in them, children will find that the more water there is above the holes, the greater the pressure forcing the water out of the holes.

## Can you move water? 20-21

Children have found that water can flow and be squirted under pressure. They now use this knowledge to help them find ways of moving water. When making a siphon, children may find it difficult to remove the air from the tube. Under supervision, they may try sucking the end of the tube until water flows.

## Will it float on water? 22-23

Children find that liquids exert an upward force on an object. This force prevents an object from sinking unless that object can exert a greater force downward. When holding a table-tennis ball under water, children will feel an upward force trying to make the ball float. Modeling clay floats if it is shaped like a boat.

## Will it move in water? 24-25

By floating the trays and pots, children form ideas about the ideal shape for an object if it is to overcome friction when moving through water. In the cork boat activity, using a larger piece of clay makes the boat more stable. Finally, by keeping the same boat hull and changing the sail, children find the best type of sail for their boat.

## Can you clean water? 26-27

Children use various filters to clean muddy water. As the filtered water could still contain harmful microbes, make sure that children do not drink it. By looking at an aquarium, children begin to see the need for clean water to support plant and animal life.